Workbook

of

The Courage to Be Disliked

A Guide to Ichiro Kishimi and Fumitake Koga's book

By TruePress Pub

Before You Start Using This Workbook...

This workbook is an unofficial companion guide to The Courage to Be Disliked by Ichiro Kishimi and Fumitake Koga. What this means is that we highly recommend that you purchase the main book before proceeding with this one.

In order to gain maximum benefits from this workbook and effectively work through each section, you need to use it along with the main book.

Here are some key tips for you:

- ✓ Approach each question with a clear mind.
- ✓ Be relaxed as you work through this book.
- ✓ Take your time while attempting each question.
- ✓ This book is a safe space for you. So, feel free to be completely honest without fear of judgement.
- ✓ Dig deep and thoroughly search yourself before answering any question.
- ✓ Faithfully apply ideas and crucial lessons.
- ✓ Get more than one copy of this workbook and attempt each section again after your initial foray to evaluate your growth. When to take another shot is completely up to you, but a period of 4 to 8 weeks is advisable.
- ✓ Remember that growth is a gradual and steady process that requires time and dedication.

What you would need:

Pen or any other writing tool. You may also consider using highlighters or sticky notes to mark vital areas as you move through each chapter.

HOW TO USE THIS WORKBOOK

This book is easy-to-use and offers an interactive guide to help you achieve maximum benefits from the main text for your personal development and growth.

As the main ideas, concepts, and models from the main book have been highlighted in this workbook, you will find that it makes it easier for you to take action and implement them.

Each chapter of this book is broken down into the following sections:

- ❖ Concise chapter-by-chapter summaries, detailing the core ideas.
- ❖ Thought-provoking exercises and questions to stretch your mind and encourage deep self-discovery, deep introspection, and growth
- ❖ Objectives & Goals of each chapter to help you achieve those milestones you have set your sights on.
- ❖ Crucial lessons and points from each chapter to help you go more in depth
- ❖ Checklist for self-assessment and accountability. The checklist section serves as a simple reminder for you to know if you have tackled each chapter appropriately.
- ❖ Action plan that helps you work out ways to practically implement areas of each chapter into your personal life.

After reading each chapter of the main book, you will be properly equipped to tackle the respective sections.

As stated earlier, we recommend attempting another copy this workbook again, so you can use the second (or third) attempt to see how differently you approached each question and how much progress you have made.

This should serve as your personal journal.

Let's go...

INTRODUCTION

This book is an in-depth exploration of a dialogue between a Greek philosopher and a youth. The layered wisdom beneath this dialogue forms the thesis of this book and its general message. Thus, the book is a compendium of philosophy delivered in relatable language for the consumption and benefit of the reader.

However, it is important to note that this book is a critical reflection of ironies laced in life but very fundamental to our growth and survival. Like the name implies, this book is a challenge to the norm, a piece of literature reserved for those willing to step into the realm of courage regardless of the societal obstacles faced.

THE FIRST NIGHT

Deny trauma

OBJECTIVES OF THIS CHAPTER
✓ To understand why people reject or deny trauma.
✓ To understand why people can change.
✓ To educate readers that trauma does not exist.

SUMMARY & OVERVIEW

This chapter discusses why people can change and why some people can't change. It also explores the correlation between Adlerian psychology and Greek philosophy; corrects some misconceptions about trauma; explains how people fabricate anger; how we can live without being controlled by our past; how people can change at any time; for us to be happy, we have to accept who we are; unhappiness is by choice and does not depend on the situation we find ourselves or what we were born into; how people choose not to change consciously and unconsciously because they are scared; and the fact that people can change by taking a firm decision to change instead of imagining it or comparing yourself with others.

The Unknown 'Third Giant'

This text talks about a Greek philosopher who is interested in psychology, how he feels that Adlerian psychology is similar to or in line with Greek philosophy, the school of psychology, the philosophy of philosophers like Alder,

Freud, and Jung, what Adlerian psychology is all about, how Alder ideas have not been fully understood yet, and concludes that the Greek philosopher theories are not developed from Greek philosophy but from the viewpoint of Adlerian psychology.

Why People Can Change

This text details the thought process of a youth who is adamant that people can't change because of his friend who wanted to change his ways, be able to go out, get a job, and hang out with people but couldn't change, and the possible reasons why he is like that. The youth further concludes that there is no effect without a cause, meaning who you become (the effect) is determined by occurrences in the past (the causes), while the philosopher argues that instead of focusing on the cause, we should let it go and focus on our present goals.

Trauma Does Not Exist

In this text, the philosopher discusses the difference between aetiology and teleology and is adamant about the fact that trauma doesn't exist. The philosopher further emphasized that in Adlerian psychology, trauma was denied and that our life is not something that is given by someone, but something we choose ourselves, and we are the ones who decide how we live. The philosopher further highlights that most of the behaviors we think are products of our trauma are merely results of the goals we set for ourselves.

People Fabricate Anger

In this text, the philosopher emphasizes that people fabricate emotions like anger for different reasons, using the youth as an example. For instance, the youth got angry at a waiter for soiling his clothes, which he wouldn't have done under normal circumstances, but due to his frustration and to fulfill his aim of making the waiter submit, he shouted and fabricated anger. However, the youth did not believe the philosopher and instead accused the philosopher of being nihilistic.

How To Live Without Being Controlled By The Past

In this text, the youth said that the philosopher is nihilistic and refuses to accept human emotions while emphasizing that emotions make use of humans. The philosopher countered his argument by saying that he believes that emotions exist and that everyone has emotions, but that doesn't mean we can't control our emotions, and we should always keep in mind that people can change.

Socrates And Adler

The philosopher talks about how everyone can change, using Socrates as an example and the first step in changing is by knowing. It also details how Socrates and Adler both conveyed their ideas through dialogue.

Are You Okay Just As You Are?

In this text, the youth talks about how he wants to be a more social person like Y and later concludes that it's not possible because they have different personalities, while the philosopher argues with him that he is not happy with himself because he does not love himself and emphasizes that we can't be reborn to be who we feel is best for us; rather, we just have to accept and be okay with who we are.

Unhappiness Is Something You Choose For Yourself

This text emphasizes the point that unhappiness is something you choose for yourself and doesn't depend on the situation you ended up in or the situation you were born into, and people choose unhappiness because it is good for them.

People Always Choose Not To Change

In this text, the philosopher attributes personality and disposition to lifestyle and further defines lifestyle as the tendencies of thought and action in life or the way one's life should be. The philosopher emphasized that we choose our personality both consciously and unconsciously around the age of 10, and we can choose to change at any time regardless of the environment, but we don't because we are scared. It also highlights some external factors that can affect our choice, which are race, nationality, culture, and home environment.

Your Life Is Decided Here And Now

The world is not as complicated as it seems, we just like to complicate things. To be able to change your lifestyle, you have to make a firm decision to change instead of imagining the change or comparing yourself with others. Changing your lifestyle is a way of giving meaning to the world and to yourself in both the way you interact with the world and your behavior.

CRUCIAL POINTS, KEY TAKEAWAYS & LESSONS

- People can change, and everyone can find happiness.
- Before an effect, there is a cause.
- We do not suffer from the shock of our experiences (trauma), but instead, we make out of them whatever suits our purposes.
- Trauma does not exist.
- We are not determined by our experiences, but the meaning we give them is self-determining.
- Emotions can be fabricated, and many people fabricate anger to achieve a particular goal.
- People are not controlled by emotions and the past.
- Unhappiness is something you choose for yourself.

EXERCISE & QUESTIONS

What does it mean to deny or reject trauma, and why do people do it?

_____

_____

_____

_____

_____

_____

_____

What led to the establishment of Adlerian psychology?

_____

_____

_____

_____

_____

_____

_____

Why were the philosopher's theories rejected?

_____

_____

_____

_____

_____

_____

_____

_____

_____

How does Adlerian psychology differ from individual psychology?

_____

_____

_____

_____

_____

_____

_____

_____

_____

Do you think Adlerian psychology is in line with Greek philosophy?

_____

_____

How is developing a theory from the viewpoint of Adlerian psychology instead of Greek philosophy beneficial to a philosopher?

How true is this statement, 'Everyone can find happiness'?

How can letting go of the cause and focusing on our future
goals help us overcome trauma?

_____

_____

_____

_____

_____

_____

_____

What is the difference between aetiology (the study of
causation) and teleology (the study of the purpose of a
given phenomenon)?

_____

_____

_____

_____

_____

_____

_____

_____

_____

What is the difference between a behavior that originates
from a goal and a behavior that originates from a cause?

_____

_____

_____

_____

_____

_____

_____

_____

_____

_____

SELF-REFLECTION

_____

_____

_____

_____

_____

_____

_____

_____

_____

_____

_____

_____

_____

_____

_____

CHECKLIST

Do you believe you were truthful in the answers above?

Yes [   ]   No [   ]   Not Really [   ]

Is there area of your personal life that this section touched?

Yes [   ]   No [   ]   Not Really [   ]

Do you think your answers would change if someone else read them?

Yes [   ]   No [   ]   Not Really [   ]

Are you ready to apply this section to your life?

Yes [   ]   No [   ]   Not Really [   ]

ACTION PLAN

Briefly outline easy steps you can start taking or one change you can make (or intend to make) in the coming days or weeks.

_____
_____
_____
_____
_____
_____
_____

THE SECOND NIGHT

All Problems Are Interpersonal Relationship Problems

OBJECTIVES OF THIS CHAPTER

✓ To understand why people dislike themselves.
✓ To understand what the feeling of inferiority is all about.
✓ To educate readers that admitting fault is not defeat.

SUMMARY & OVERVIEW

This chapter discusses the reason why people don't love themselves; why and how all the problems we have are as a result of interpersonal relationships; what would happen if we lived in a world without interpersonal relationships; the origin of the feeling of inferiority; how the feeling of inferiority is a subjective interpretation and not an objective fact; how inferior complex is an excuse; the differences between the feeling of inferiority and inferiority complex; the correlation between inferiority and superiority complex; how human beings are equal even if we are not the same; the connection between the feeling of superiority, interpersonal relationships, and competition; how power struggle can lead to revenge; how to overcome the tasks we face in life, and the need to face every relationship instead of avoiding, running, or putting off dealing with it.

Why You Dislike Yourself

This text discusses low self-esteem as the reason why many people don't like themselves and don't see the good in anything they do. The author argues that instead of trying to change who you are or what you don't like about yourself, accept yourself the way you are, regardless of the outcome, and have the courage to move forward. It emphasizes that one of the reasons why we start disliking ourselves is because we are scared of being disliked by others or getting hurt in interpersonal relationships. However, we should always keep in mind that it is impossible to not get hurt in our relations with other people.

All Problems Are Interpersonal Relationship Problems

This section talks about loneliness, what brings loneliness, why we are lonely, and how we can't do without interpersonal relationships. It further emphasizes that the cause of all the problems in the world is interpersonal relationships, and the world will be a better place and will not be lonely if the interpersonal relationship was not there in the first place.

Feelings Of Inferiority Are Subjective Assumptions

This text talks about the feelings of inferiority and what they are all about. It highlights that the feelings of inferiority that we are suffering from are subjective interpretations, not objective facts, and that subjectivity gives us the right to choose our lifestyle. It further concludes that the feelings of inferiority stem from interpersonal relationship.

An Inferiority Complex Is An Excuse

In this text, the philosopher discusses the pursuit of superiority as the counterpart of the feeling of inferiority and emphasizes that the feeling of inferiority and the pursuit of superiority are not diseases but are healthy and can promote striving and growth if used in the right way.

Braggarts Have Feelings Of Inferiority

In this text, the philosopher and the youth discuss the feeling of inferiority as a condition of feeling some sort of lack in oneself in the present situation. The conversation further details how this lack can be filled up, how the inferiority complex can develop into a superiority complex, and various examples of superiority complex and the feeling of inferiority. In conclusion, the inferiority complex and superiority complex might seem like opposites, but in actuality, they border on each other.

Life Is Not A Competition

The text discusses the pursuit of superiority and defines it as the mindset of taking a single step forward on one's own feet, not the mindset of competition of the kind that necessitates aiming to be greater than other people, while emphasizing that life is not competition. It also talks about what a healthy feeling of inferiority involves and highlights that although we are different, we are all equal.

You're The Only One Worrying About Your Appearance.

In this text, the philosopher talks about the connection between the feeling of superiority, interpersonal relationships, and competition, emphasizing that when one is conscious of competition, victory, and defeat, it is inevitable that feelings of inferiority will arise because one is constantly comparing oneself to others and the disadvantages of competing.

From Power Struggle To Revenge

In this text, the youth talks about his disagreement with the philosopher on various topics that have been previously discussed, like teleology, the fact that trauma does not exist, people fabricating anger, etc., while the philosopher talks about the differences between personal grudges and righteous indignation, how getting angry can make you lose the power struggle, and how power struggle can lead to revenge.

Admitting Fault Is Not Defeat

This text highlights ways in which we can handle situations without being angry or sulk up emotions that arise from them. It further details anger as a form of communication, the importance of communication without anger, and, in conclusion, the philosopher's advice that admitting mistakes, conveying words of apology, and stepping down from power struggles is not defeat.

Overcoming The Tasks That Face You In Life

This text highlights that there are two objectives for behavior, which are to be self-reliant and to live in harmony with society, and that there are two objectives for the psychology that supports these behaviors, which are the consciousness that I have the ability and the consciousness that people are my comrades. It also talks about how we can achieve these objectives by facing what Adler calls 'life tasks,' which are divided into tasks of work, tasks of friendship, and tasks of love, and how we can overcome these tasks.

Red String And Rigid Chains

This text talks about the tasks of friendship, emphasizing that there's no value at all in the number of friends or acquaintances you have. It further talks about the tasks of love, which is divided into love relationships and relationships with family. It also explores how a friend relationship can turn into love, what real love is all about, and the need for us not to run, avoid, or put off dealing with a relationship, no matter how distressing it may be.

Don't Fall For The 'Life-Lie'

This text talks about the things we do to avoid interpersonal relationships, the consequences of avoiding life tasks and clinging to life-lies, emphasizing that the fact that you are avoiding your life tasks and clinging to your life-lies isn't because you are steeped in evil, nor is it an issue of being condemned from a moralistic standpoint, but that it is an issue of courage.

From The Psychology Of Possession To The Psychology Of Practice

In this text, the philosopher emphasizes that Adlerian psychology is not a 'psychology of possession', but a 'psychology of use' meaning it's not what one is born with, but what use one makes of that equipment.

CRUCIAL POINTS, KEY TAKEAWAYS & LESSONS

- Admitting wrong is a good attitude.
- It is impossible to not get hurt in your relations with other people.
- Loneliness is having other people, society, and community around you and having a deep sense of being excluded from them.
- All problems are interpersonal relationship problems.
- Life is not a competition.
- The inferiority complex and the superiority complex are extensions of competition.
- Admitting fault is not defeat.
- The one who boasts does so only out of a feeling of inferiority.

Exercise & Questions

What are the advantages of you liking yourself?

_____
_____
_____
_____
_____
_____
_____

What causes low self-esteem, and how can it be remedied?

_____
_____
_____
_____
_____
_____
_____
_____
_____

Why do people dislike and view themselves with low self-esteem?

_____
_____

_____

_____

_____

_____

_____

_____

_____

_____

Why do you focus only on your shortcomings, and why
have you decided not to start liking yourself?

_____

_____

_____

_____

_____

_____

_____

_____

_____

How true is this statement, "All problems are
interpersonal relationship problems"?

_____

_____

_____

_____

_____

_____

_____

_____

_____

_____

From personal experience, how true do you think this
statement is that in order to feel lonely, we need other
people?

_____

_____

_____

_____

_____

_____

_____

What do you think will happen in a world where there are
no interpersonal relationships?

_____

_____

_____

_____

_____

_____

_____

_____
_____
_____
_____
_____
_____
_____
_____

How does Adlerian psychology advise us to overcome the life tasks of work, friendship, and love?

_____
_____
_____
_____
_____
_____
_____
_____

What is the correlation between interpersonal relationships and feelings of inferiority?

_____
_____
_____
_____
_____
_____
_____

_____

_____

_____

_____

_____

_____

_____

From your personal experience, do you agree with the
philosopher that feelings of inferiority originate from
interpersonal relationships?

_____

_____

_____

_____

_____

_____

SELF-REFLECTION

_____

_____

_____

_____

_____

_____

_____

_____

CHECKLIST

Do you believe you were truthful in the answers above?

Yes ☐   No ☐   Not Really ☐

Is there area of your personal life that this section touched?

Yes ☐   No ☐   Not Really ☐

Do you think your answers would change if someone else read them?

Yes ☐   No ☐   Not Really ☐

Are you ready to apply this section to your life?

Yes ☐   No ☐   Not Really ☐

ACTION PLAN

Briefly outline easy steps you can start taking or one change you can make (or intend to make) in the coming days or weeks.

_____

_____

_____

_____

_____

_____

_____

THE THIRD NIGHT

Discard Other People's Task

OBJECTIVES OF THIS CHAPTER

- ✓ To know how to separate tasks.
- ✓ To know the consequences of living your life for others.
- ✓ To understand the need for separation of tasks.

SUMMARY & OVERVIEW

The chapter discusses the need for us to let go of our desire to be recognized by others; to not live our lives to satisfy the expectations of others; the need for task separation; how to separate tasks; why we should discard the tasks of other people; how we can get rid of interpersonal relationship problems; build an interpersonal relationship while practicing separation of tasks; how the desire for recognition makes us un-free; and what real freedom is.

Deny the Desire For Recognition

This text talks about money as a possible source of freedom. It further highlights interpersonal relationships as the only thing money can't buy, while emphasizing the bad and the good side of interpersonal relationship, how humans desire recognition, and how Adlerian psychology states that there is no need to be recognized by others.

Do Not Live To Satisfy The Expectations Of Others.

The text talks about why people seek recognition, which in most cases is due to the influence of reward-and-punishment education, meaning that if one takes appropriate action, one receives praise, but if one takes inappropriate action, one receives punishment. It also discusses the consequences of seeking recognition from others and emphasizes that we shouldn't live to satisfy other people's expectations.

How to Separate Tasks

This text talks about the need to separate tasks, how to separate our tasks from other people's tasks, and the consequences of intruding on other people's tasks.

Discard Other People's Tasks

This text advises us to draw a line with people, including family, while consciously discarding the tasks of other people and keeping in mind that you are not to live your life for others and that they are not to live their life for you, even if it's your children. The text also highlights the need for us to believe in others (partners, children, etc.), keeping in mind that belief is a separation task and the advantages of discarding other people's tasks.

How To Rid Yourself Of Interpersonal Relationship Problems

This text discusses how we can get rid of interpersonal relationships, with the first step being to do the separation task, and emphasizes that what others think about you is not important and you just have to do what you feel is best for you and what you believe in.

Cut the Gordian Knot

In this text, the philosopher talks about the possibility of building an interpersonal relationship while practicing separation of tasks, and it further emphasizes that it is possible because separation of tasks is the gateway to interpersonal relationships as it lends a hand when needed but does not encroach on the person's territory.

Desire for Recognition Makes You Unfree

This text talks about the disadvantages of living a life to please others or to gain the recognition of others. It further highlights how living your life for others can make us unfree, and how living for yourself can bring freedom.

What Real Freedom Is

The text defines real freedom as an attitude akin to pushing up one's tumbling self from below and emphasizes that even though the desire for recognition is natural, it can be controlled, and it's only when we have controlled it that we can experience real freedom.

You Hold the Cards To Interpersonal Relationships

This text advises us to always keep in mind that the card to interpersonal relationships is in our hands and can only be in other people's minds when we desire recognition from others.

CRUCIAL POINTS, KEY TAKEAWAYS & LESSONS

- Do not live to satisfy the expectations of others.
- You are the only one who can change yourself.
- Don't expect your partner or children to live their lives for you.
- What others think about you and what sort of judgment they pass on you does not matter.
- Destiny is not something brought about by legend but by clearing away with one's sword.
- Not wanting to be disliked by others is an instinctive or impulsive desire.
- Separation of tasks is the gateway to interpersonal relationships.

EXERCISE & QUESTIONS

From your perspective, what do you think is the meaning and source of freedom, and why can't people be free?

_____
_____
_____
_____
_____
_____
_____
_____
_____
_____
_____

What is the true nature of whatever it is that is constraining you?

_____
_____
_____
_____
_____
_____
_____
_____
_____
_____

How true do you think this statement is, 'Money is coined freedom'?

_____
_____
_____
_____
_____
_____
_____
_____
_____
_____

What is it about your interpersonal relationships that is preventing you from attaining freedom?

_____
_____
_____
_____
_____
_____
_____
_____
_____

Why do you seek recognition from others?

_____
_____
_____

_____

_____

_____

_____

_____

_____

_____

_____

_____

Why do we need to separate our tasks from other people's tasks?

_____

_____

_____

_____

_____

_____

_____

_____

_____

What happens when you intervene in other people's tasks?

_____

_____

_____

_____

_____

_____

_____

_____

_____

_____

How can we rid ourselves of interpersonal relationship problems?

_____

_____

_____

_____

_____

_____

_____

_____

What happened to you previously that you think if you had applied the separation task, the outcome would be different?

_____

_____

_____

_____

_____

_____

_____

_____

How can one build good interpersonal relationships while practicing separation tasks?

_____
_____
_____
_____
_____
_____
_____
_____
_____
_____
_____
_____

SELF-REFLECTION

_____
_____
_____
_____
_____
_____
_____
_____
_____
_____
_____
_____

CHECKLIST

Do you believe you were truthful in the answers above?

Yes [ ]   No [ ]   Not Really [ ]

Is there area of your personal life that this section touched?

Yes [ ]   No [ ]   Not Really [ ]

Do you think your answers would change if someone else read them?

Yes [ ]   No [ ]   Not Really [ ]

Are you ready to apply this section to your life?

Yes [ ]   No [ ]   Not Really [ ]

ACTION PLAN

Briefly outline easy steps you can start taking or one change you can make (or intend to make) in the coming days or weeks.

_____

_____

_____

_____

_____

_____

_____

THE FORTH NIGHT

Where The Centre Of The World Is

OBJECTIVES OF THIS CHAPTER

- ✓ To understand how interpersonal relations are viewed in Adlerian psychology and community feelings.
- ✓ To know the kind of relationships we should form with others.
- ✓ To educate readers on where the center of the world is.

SUMMARY & OVERVIEW

This chapter talks about the correlation between separation of tasks; individual psychology and holism; the goal of interpersonal relationships; what self-centeredness is all about; we are not the center of the world even though we are our life protagonists; the importance of creating awareness for large and multiple communities; don't rebuke or praise; the difference between assistance and intervention; and how to feel you have value.

Individual Psychology and Holism

This text talks about how separation of tasks is more of individualism (I am I and You are You). It also details separation of tasks as a way of thinking with which to unravel the threads of the complex entanglement of one's interpersonal relation and not keeping other people away, separation of tasks as a prescription for resolving interpersonal relationship problems, and how interpersonal relations do not end because we separated tasks.

The Goal of Interpersonal Relationships Is A Feeling Of Community

This text discusses the goal of interpersonal relationships, which is to form a community, how to form that community, and what that community consists of. It also emphasizes that the community is not merely one of the pre-existing frameworks that the word might bring to mind but is also inclusive of literally everything—the entire universe, from the past to the future.

Why Am I Only Interested In Myself?

This text discusses what it means to be self-centered and defines self-centered people as people who are incapable of carrying out the separation of tasks, and who are obsessed with the desire for recognition. It also talks about why people are self-centered.

You Are Not the Center of the World

This text emphasizes that the fact that you are the protagonist of your life does not mean you are the center of the world. It also talks about how one can feel a sense of belonging, the importance of commitment to a community, and the importance of community.

Listen to the Voice of A Larger Community

This text is trying to educate us that we belong to a separate, larger community that is beyond the one you see in your immediate vicinity and that you are contributing in some way within that community. It also talks about why we need to belong to a community and why we need to be aware of large and multiple communities. In conclusion, do not cling to the small community right in front of you because there will always be more 'you and I', and more 'everyone', and larger communities that exist.

Do Not Rebuke or Praise

This text discusses how carrying out the separation of tasks connects with good relations and the approaches to use to speak when raising people, which are by rebuke and by praise. It further says that during childrearing, Adlerian psychology takes a stance that one must not praise or rebuke, and it explains why Adlerian psychology took that stance.

The Encouragement Approach

This text talks about what intervention is all about, why we should avoid intervention, and the difference between assistance and intervention. It also emphasizes that we should offer assistance that does not turn into intervention, neither praises nor rebukes; instead, we should offer assistance that is based on horizontal relationships, which is referred to as encouragement in Adlerian psychology, the consequences of praise and rebuke, and steps to take to not live up life for others.

How To Feel You Have Value

This text talks about the importance of not judging other people, as judgment is created by vertical relationships, defines praise as one receiving judgment from another person as 'good', what a person must do to get courage, and when a person will be able to feel he has worth.

Exist In The Present

This text talks about how we can be of use to others by just being there, the reason for gratitude, why we should be grateful at all times, and emphasizes that people can be of use to someone else simply by being alive and having a true sense of their worth just by being alive. In conclusion, someone has to start; other people might not be cooperative, but that is not connected to you.

People Cannot Make Proper Use Of Self

This text talks about why people do not feel that you have worth, how you can increase your worth by first building a horizontal relationship between yourself and another person, the importance of building either a horizontal or vertical relationship, and how to build a horizontal relationship.

CRUCIAL POINTS, KEY TAKEAWAYS & LESSONS

- Separation of tasks does not lead to the end of interpersonal relationships.
- Separation of tasks can resolve interpersonal relationship problems.
- Interpersonal relations can be a source of happiness or unhappiness.
- Community feeling is also referred to as social interest.
- People who are obsessed with recognition are not looking at others but themselves.
- The fact that there are people who do not think well of you is proof that you are living in freedom.
- We belong to a separate, larger community that is beyond the one you see in your immediate vicinity.

EXERCISE & QUESTIONS

Why is Adlerian's psychology called an individual psychology?

_____

_____

_____

_____

_____

_____

_____

_____

_____

_____

What is the goal of interpersonal relationships?

_____
_____
_____
_____
_____
_____
_____
_____
_____
_____
_____

How can the separation of tasks improve your
interpersonal relationships?

_____
_____
_____
_____
_____
_____
_____
_____

How is the goal of interpersonal relationships a community
feeling?

_____
_____

_____
_____
_____
_____
_____
_____
_____
_____

Considering the chapter, what kind of relationship should
we form with others?

_____
_____
_____
_____
_____
_____
_____

Why can it be said that interpersonal relations can bring
you happiness and unhappiness?

_____
_____
_____
_____
_____
_____

What does it mean for one to be self-centered?

_____
_____
_____
_____
_____
_____
_____

How can one attain a sense of belonging?

_____
_____
_____
_____
_____
_____
_____

Why is it important to belong to a community and to be
aware of large, multiple communities?

_____
_____
_____
_____
_____
_____
_____

How can one build interpersonal relations with this separation of tasks, and arrive in the end at the community feeling that 'it's okay to be here'?

_____
_____
_____
_____
_____
_____
_____
_____
_____

SELF-REFLECTION

_____
_____
_____
_____
_____
_____
_____
_____
_____
_____
_____
_____

CHECKLIST

Do you believe you were truthful in the answers above?

Yes [ ]   No [ ]   Not Really [ ]

Is there area of your personal life that this section touched?

Yes [ ]   No [ ]   Not Really [ ]

Do you think your answers would change if someone else read them?

Yes [ ]   No [ ]   Not Really [ ]

Are you ready to apply this section to your life?

Yes [ ]   No [ ]   Not Really [ ]

ACTION PLAN

Briefly outline easy steps you can start taking or one change you can make (or intend to make) in the coming days or weeks.

_____

_____

_____

_____

_____

_____

_____

THE FIFTH NIGHT

To Live In Earnest In The Here And Now

OBJECTIVES OF THIS CHAPTER

- ✓ To understand how we can live earnestly.
- ✓ To understand the difference between self-affirmation and self-acceptance.
- ✓ To understand the importance of self-acceptance, confidence in others, and contribution to others in building a community.

SUMMARY & OVERVIEW

This chapter talks about how excessive self-consciousness can hinder our growth; the importance of self-acceptance; confidence in others; and contribution to others in building a community; the difference between trust and confidence; the importance of contribution to others; the consequences of not living a harmonious life; the courage to be normal; the meaning of life; and why we should and how we can live our life earnestly here and now.

Excessive Self-Consciousness Stifles the Self

This text talks about why we worry about ourselves, how we know when we are excessively self-conscious, and how excessive self-consciousness can hinder us.

Not Self-Affirmation—Self-Acceptance

This text talks about the things needed to gain community feeling, which are self-acceptance, confidence in others, and contribution to others. It emphasizes that there is no need to be positive or affirm oneself (self-affirmation); instead, we should practice self-acceptance, and highlights the differences between self-affirmation and self-acceptance.

The Difference Between Trust and Confidence

The text discusses the difference between trust and confidence, the need for confidence in others when one is switching from attachment to self to concern for others, what confidence entails, the goal of confidence, and the importance of self-acceptance.

The Essence of Work Is a Contribution to the Common Good

The text talks about how community feeling cannot be attained only by self-acceptance and confidence in others, but also by contribution to others, what contribution to others is all about, the need for contribution, and the essence of work.

Young People Walk Ahead Of Adults

The text talks about how and when contribution can be carried out, emphasizing that contribution that is carried out while one is seeing other people as enemies may indeed lead to hypocrisy. It also talks about the connection between self-acceptance, confidence in others, and contribution to others.

Workaholism Is A Life-Lie

This text highlights the consequences of living a life without harmony and emphasizes that living that is lacking in 'harmony of life'. It is a way of living in which one sees only a part of things but judges the whole. It also exposes the consequences of being a workaholic and emphasizes that, in a sense, workaholic is a way of living where one refuses to acknowledge one's life tasks.

You Can Be Happy Now

This text talks about what happiness is to human beings, which is contribution to others, and the greatest unhappiness being not being able to like oneself, and how one can get a feeling of contribution. In conclusion, the fact that all human beings can be happy doesn't mean that every human being is happy.

Two Paths Traveled By Those Wanting To Be 'special Beings'

The text talks about things that people do, whether bad or good, to attract the attention of other people, get out of the 'normal' condition, and become a 'special being'.

The Courage To Be Normal

The text talks about why people want to be special instead of normal, why we should be normal, how to be normal, why people reject normality, and why we need the courage to be normal.

Life Is A Series Of Moments

This text talks about how we see life and emphasizes that we should not treat it as a line; instead, we should think of life as a series of dots. If you look through a magnifying glass at a solid line drawn with chalk, you will discover that what you thought was a line is a series of small dots. Seemingly linear existence is a series of dots; in other words, life is a series of moments.

Live Like You're Dancing.

The text emphasizes that we should think of life as a series of moments in which one lives as if one were dancing right now, around and around each passing instant.

Shine A Light On The Here And Now

This text emphasizes that we should live more earnestly only here and now, not to dwell on the past, or predict the future. In conclusion, we should always remember that life is a series of moments, and neither the past nor the future exists.

The Greatest Life-Lie

The text talks about why we should live life earnestly here and now instead of living in the past or predicting the future, and further advises us that living earnestly doesn't mean that we should be serious because life is always simple, not something that one needs to get too serious about.

Give Meaning To Seemingly Meaningless Life

The text discusses the meaning of life and later concludes that life has no general meaning because its meaning has to be assigned to it by the individual. It also takes a look at what people live for, why the meaning of life has to be assigned to it by the individual, why people are lost in life, and the nature of an energetic life. In conclusion, always keep in mind that if I change, the world will change. No one else will change the world for you, and you should start. With no regard to whether others are cooperative or not.

CRUCIAL POINTS, KEY TAKEAWAYS & LESSONS

- Anyone can behave like a king when they are alone.
- The important thing is not what one is born with, but what use one makes of that thing.
- We do not lack ability; we just lack courage, and it all comes down to courage.
- In Adlerian psychology, the basis of interpersonal relations is not founded on trust but on confidence.
- Unconditional confidence is a means for making your interpersonal relationship with a person better, and for building a horizontal relationship.
- Contribution to others does not connote self-sacrifice.
- We become aware of our worth only when we feel that our existence and behavior are beneficial to the community.

- Contribution that is carried out while one is seeing other people as enemies may indeed lead to hypocrisy.

EXERCISE & QUESTIONS

What are the consequences of excessive self-consciousness?

_____
_____
_____
_____
_____
_____
_____
_____
_____
_____
_____

Why should we stop being attached to the 'I' and make the switch to 'concern for others'?

_____
_____
_____
_____
_____
_____
_____
_____

How do you know when you are excessively self-conscious?

_____
_____
_____
_____
_____
_____
_____
_____

According to this section, what do you think is the meaning of happiness?

_____
_____
_____
_____
_____
_____
_____
_____
_____

What is the difference between self-affirmation and self-acceptance?

_____
_____

From your point of view, is there any need for affirmative resignation?

What is the essence of work?

How does trust differ from confidence?

_____
_____
_____
_____
_____
_____
_____
_____
_____
_____

What role does unconditional confidence play in building a
horizontal relationship?

_____
_____
_____
_____
_____
_____
_____
_____
_____
_____
_____

What is the correlation between self-acceptance,
confidence in others, and contribution to others?

_____
_____
_____
_____
_____
_____
_____
_____
_____
_____
_____
_____
_____
_____

SELF-REFLECTION

_____
_____
_____
_____
_____
_____
_____
_____
_____
_____
_____
_____
_____

CHECKLIST

Do you believe you were truthful in the answers above?

Yes ☐   No ☐   Not Really ☐

Is there area of your personal life that this section touched?

Yes ☐   No ☐   Not Really ☐

Do you think your answers would change if someone else read them?

Yes ☐   No ☐   Not Really ☐

Are you ready to apply this section to your life?

Yes ☐   No ☐   Not Really ☐

ACTION PLAN

Briefly outline easy steps you can start taking or one change you can make (or intend to make) in the coming days or weeks.

_____

_____

_____

_____

_____

_____